YOUR KNOWLEDGE HAS VALUE

- We will publish your bachelor's and master's thesis, essays and papers

- Your own eBook and book - sold worldwide in all relevant shops

- Earn money with each sale

Upload your text at www.GRIN.com and publish for free

Bibliographic information published by the German National Library:

The German National Library lists this publication in the National Bibliography; detailed bibliographic data are available on the Internet at http://dnb.dnb.de .

This book is copyright material and must not be copied, reproduced, transferred, distributed, leased, licensed or publicly performed or used in any way except as specifically permitted in writing by the publishers, as allowed under the terms and conditions under which it was purchased or as strictly permitted by applicable copyright law. Any unauthorized distribution or use of this text may be a direct infringement of the author s and publisher s rights and those responsible may be liable in law accordingly.

Imprint:

Copyright © 2017 GRIN Verlag, Open Publishing GmbH
Print and binding: Books on Demand GmbH, Norderstedt Germany
ISBN: 9783668608481

This book at GRIN:

https://www.grin.com/document/379548

Kadri Ouahab, Abdelhadi Adel

Relational database courses and exercises

GRIN Publishing

GRIN - Your knowledge has value

Since its foundation in 1998, GRIN has specialized in publishing academic texts by students, college teachers and other academics as e-book and printed book. The website www.grin.com is an ideal platform for presenting term papers, final papers, scientific essays, dissertations and specialist books.

Visit us on the internet:

http://www.grin.com/

http://www.facebook.com/grincom

http://www.twitter.com/grin_com

Relational database courses and exercises
Dr. KADRI Ouahab
Dr. ABDELHADI Adel

Contents

Contents 2
Introduction 5
1.1. Database 6
    1.1.1. Definition 6
    1.1.2. The description of a database 6
        1.1.2.1. Definitions 6
1.2. Database Management System 6
    1.2.1. Definition 6
    1.2.2. The aims and properties of these systems are manifold 7
    2.1. Introduction 8
    2.2. basic concepts 8
        2.2.1. Attribute 8
        2.2.2. Field 8
        2.2.3. Schematic relationship 8
        2.2.4. Relationship 8
        2.2.5. Degree 8
        2.2.6. Occurrence 8
        2.2.7. cardinality 9
        2.2.8. candidate key 9
        2.2.9. primary key 9
        2.2.10. foreign key 9
2.3. relational model 9
    2.3.1. Translation of the conceptual model into relational model 9
        2.3.1.1. Rules passages MC objects NCM Relations 9
        2.3.1.2. passing rules of associations MC NCM Relations 9
3.1. The basic operations 12
3.2. Expression of the relational algebra 15
4.1. functional dependence 17
    4.1.1. Introduction 17
    4.1.2. Definition 17
    4.1.3. Graphical representation of functional dependencies 17
    4.1.4. Properties (Armstrong axioms) 18
    4.1.5. elementary functional dependence 18
    4.1.6. direct functional dependence 18
4.2. The transitive closure 18
4.3. The minimum coverage 18
4.4. Closure of a set of attributes 19
    4.4.1. Definition 19
    4.4.2. A closure algorithm 19
4.5. Research Process key candidates 20

4.6. poor design 21
4.7. The decomposition 23
    4.7.1. Definition 23
    4.7.2. Decomposition Lossless Information 24
    4.7.3. Decomposition without loss of DF 24
4.8. Why normalize? 25
    4.8.1 First Normal Form 25
    4.8.2. Second Normal Form 25
    4.8.3. Third Normal Form 26
    4.8.4. normal form Boyce-Codd 26
    4.9 Decomposition into 3NF 27
    4.10. valid decomposition BCNF 28
4.11. Decomposition without loss of information: Ullman algorithm 29
    4.11.1. Formalism of the algorithm: 29
    4.11.2. Sample Application 30
5.1. Basic Structure 31
    Select clause 5.1.2 31
    5.1.3. Where clause 31
    5.1.4. The From clause 32
    5.1.5. The variables tuples 32
    5.1.6. The Order by clause 32
    5.1.7 set operators 32
5.2. The aggregate functions 33
    5.2.1 aggregates and group by 33
    5.2.2. Aggregates and the having clause 33
    5.2.3. nested queries 33
    5.2.4. The views 35
    5.2.5. Changing relationships 35
5.3. Sql as ldd 36
    5.3.1. Areas 36
    5.3.2. Creating tables 37
    5.3.3. Schema Manipulation 37
    5.3.4. foreign key 37
    5.3.5. outer join 39
    5.3.6. Mechanism of Rights 39
    5.3.7. The rights in sql 39
    5.3.8. Using Views 40
TP 1: Creating the database 41
TP 2: Inserting data 41
TP 3: Importing and exporting data 42
TP 4: Selecting Data 42
TP 5: Data Update 43

TP 6: Data Deletion 43
TP 7: Relations between tables 44
Exercises 46
Exercises Solutions 53

Introduction

This course is intended for computing sophomores and aims at presenting basic principles of relational DBMS and the practice of these fundamentals. The course content is mainly the following:

Chapter 1: Introduction to databases
Chapter 2: Relational Model
Chapter 3: Relational Algebra
Chapter 4: Standardization
Chapter 5: SQL Language
Chapter 6: Practical work

A set of exercises are included at the end of the document. We added a tutorial section and directed to allow students to apply the concepts learned in the five chapters.

For any questions or suggestions, you can contact me by email at the following address:

ouahabk@yahoo.fr

1. Introduction to databases
1.1. Database
1.1.1. Definition
A database is a set of interrelated information stored on a storage medium accessible by one or more applications, without duplication and structured independently of any application to meet the needs of different users. [3]

Example:

In a university details: students, teachers, courses presented and general resources can be pooled and made available to many users (teaching service, training services, scientific advice etc.).

1.1.2. The description of a database
1.1.2.1. Definitions
1. A schema is simply a description of the data in the database. This description is consistent with a data model that offers descriptive tools (structures, constraints and operations).
2. An instance is the actual content of the database at a given time.

The description of a database is done at three levels [1]:

1. External level: This level concerns the definition of types of users who can each have a separate view of the same base. Each of these views is derived from the conceptual schema.
2. The Internal or physical level: this level is relative to the developers. Physical data organization and access functions are defined (file organization, index, structure ...).
3. The conceptual level includes all external views without seeking how to save the data (abstract description).

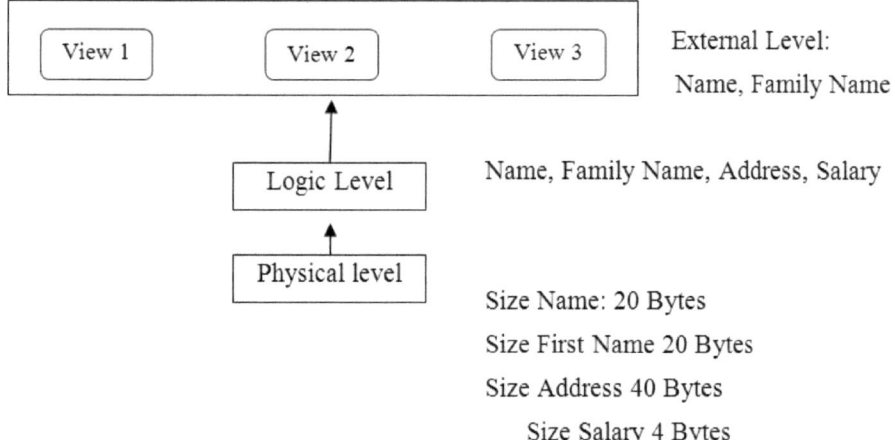

1.2. Database Management System
1.2.1. Definition
DBMS or Data Base Management System is a software system for storing and sharing information in a database, ensuring the quality, sustainability and the confidentiality of information while hiding the complexity of operations (wikipedia).

1.2.2. The aims and properties of these systems are manifold

- ➢ Give a description of the information stored in the database (you must ensure independence between the data and programs that process). [8]
- ➢ Provide an interface to ensure interaction with the database (search, update, delete).
- ➢ Providing a data manipulation language (DML) to allow the user to make requests to manipulate the databases.
- ➢ Guarantee the physical and logical data independence: the user does not have to know the physical organization of data (sequential access indexed sequential ...) and their logical organization. A change from the implantation of the base should not have any effect on the requests of the user. This independence allows in particular to offer several partial views of the same base in different types of users.
- ➢ Minimize the presence of unnecessary redundancy.

There are two types of redundancy:

1. The same data is present multiple times in different files.
2. Data is physically present in a file but can be inferred from other data.

- ➢ Maintaining data consistency through centralized administration supported by the Data Base Administrator (DBA) (validity of data, data dependency ...). These include for example the case:

1. Compulsory redundancy when the update will be "complete" to ensure consistency of the database.
2. Checking integrity constraints that must be constantly checked to ensure consistency of the database. They are verified during updates tuples: value to be necessarily defined range of possible values, typing ...

- ➢ Providing multiple access to the data and address the problem of concurrency (the problem of mutual exclusion in, for example, the update "simultaneous").
- ➢ Guaranteeing the security of data access (confidentiality, identification of users).
- ➢ Manage opportunities failures and make them transparent to the user (checkpoint).
- ➢ Provide efficient access to data.

Among the existing DBMS include: Oracle, Ingres, SQL Server, O2, Access, DB2, MySql, MSQL, PostgreSQL

2. Relational model
2.1. Introduction
The relational model is a way to model data in a database that is based on mathematical principles put forward by Codd in 1970 [9].
2.2. basic concepts
2.2.1. Attribute
Definition: An attribute is an identifier (name) describing a recorded data in a database.

Example :

The registration number and the name of a student are attributes.

2.2.2. Field
Definition: The domain of an attribute is the set, finite or infinite, its possible values.

Example :

The registration number attribute field for all combinations of five numbers and domain name for all combinations of letters (string).

2.2.3. Schematic relationship
Definition: A relation schema R, indicated R (A1: D1, A2: D2, ..., An: Dn) is an attribute group. Each attribute Ai is the name of a role played by the domain Di in the relation schema R.

A relation schema R is used to describe a relationship.

Example :

Student (num_insc: Integer, name: String, name: String). We can also write the scheme as follows: Student (num_insc, name).

2.2.4. Relationship
Definition: A relation is a subset of the Cartesian product of n domains attribute (n> 0).

A relationship is represented as a two-dimensional array in which the n attributes included titles of n columns. An example of relationship with three attributes:

num_insc	name	first name
00001	Sid Ali	sakina
00011	Ben Mohamad	Fatima zahra
00012	Ben Ali	Zine alabidine
00003	Ali	whip

Student (num_insc: Integer, name: String, name: String).

2.2.5. Degree
Definition: The degree of a relationship is the number of attributes, such as the degree the student relationship is 3.

2.2.6. Occurrence
definition: An instance is a member of the set represented by a relationship.

In other words, a case is a line of the table. For example the triple (00003 Ali, whip).

2.2.7. cardinality

Definition: The cardinality of a relationship is the number of occurrences. For example, the cardinality of the relationship is 4 student.

2.2.8. candidate key

Definition: A candidate key of a relationship is a minimum set of relationship attributes that indexes each line in a differentiated manner.

- ➢ The value of a candidate key is to separate all occurrences.
- ➢ The candidate keys of a relationship does not necessarily have the same number of attributes.
- ➢ A candidate key can be formed of an arbitrary attribute, used only for this purpose.

2.2.9. primary key

Definition : The primary key of a relationship is one of its key candidates.

- ➢ The primary key can be selected in a random manner but the context often helps determine which candidate key is to be considered as the primary key.
- ➢ Generally, the attributes that form the primary key is stressed.

Example :

Student (Code_per, Name, Surname, Address, Date_nais, Lieu_nais, Num_ASS)

Identify all the key candidates? What is the primary key that you can choose?

2.2.10. foreign key

definition: A foreign key of a relationship is formed of one or more attributes that make up a key in another relationship.

Example :

Student (No. ETUD, name, age);

Courses (NAMEC, schedule, prof);

Follows (# N ° ETUD, #NameC).

2.3. relational model

2.3.1. Translation of the conceptual model into relational model

Entities and associations have resulted in relationships. [2]

2.3.1.1. Rules passages MC objects NCM Relations

1. Any object MC turns into relationship in the MR;
2. All object properties become attributes of the relationship;
3. The ID of the object becomes the key to the relationship.

2.3.1.2. passing rules of associations MC NCM Relations

Case 1: type cardinality (x, 1), (x, n) in a binary combination.

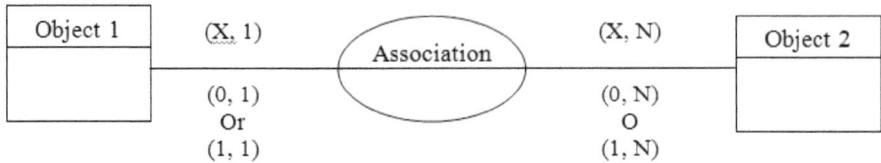

1. The object 1 becomes the R1 relationship
2. The object 2 is the relationship R2
3. The object identifier 2 becomes an attribute of the relationship R1, it will be called foreign key.
4. The properties of the association become R attributes.

Example:

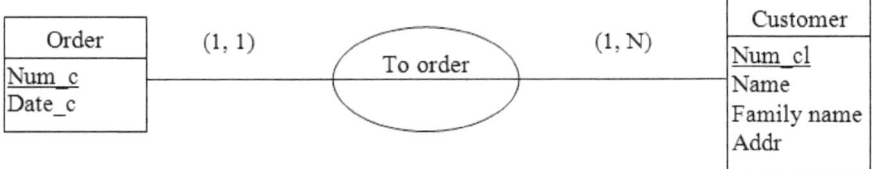

Customer (Num_cl, Name, family name, addr)

Order (Num_c, Date_c, #Num_cl).

Case 2: Type cardinality (X, N), (X, N) in combination with any degree.

1. All objects become relations
2. The association is a relationship,
3. The identifier of the Association the key to the relationship,
4. The properties of the association become the relationship attributes.

Example :

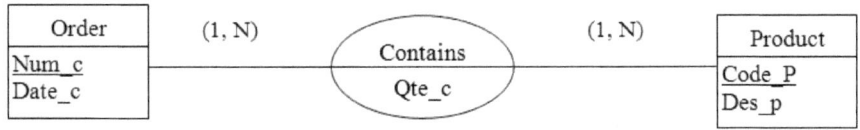

Order (Num_c, Date_c)

Product (Code_P, Des_p)

Contains (#Num_c, #Code_P, Qte_c).

Special cases :

(X, 1), (X, 1):

Id 1 becomes foreign key in the relationship associated with O2;
Id 2 is a foreign key in the relationship associated with O1

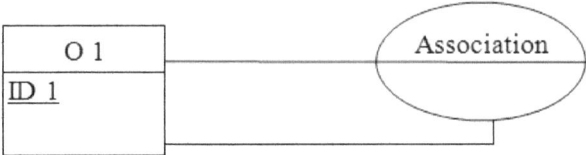

A) *Case reflexive association:*

R1 (ID_1, # ID_1).
Example :

Item (Num_p, Des, #Num_P_Cible).

3. Relational Algebra
3.1. The basic operations

The relational algebra can meet the requests because (theorem) any query can be formulated from the following [10, 11].

The union is binary operations (tables = tuple sets):
- corresponding to the usual operations of set theory
- can be applied on the same table schema and gives a new same pattern table

- **The union**

The union is binary operations (tables = tuple sets):
- corresponding to the usual operations of set theory
- can be applied on the same table schema and gives a new same pattern table

R	A	B	C
	a	e	f
	b	c	d
	f	g	e

S	A	B	C
	i	h	g
	b	d	c

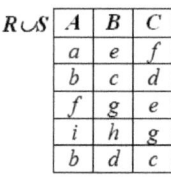

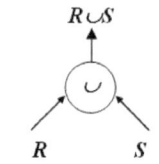

Graphical notation

- **the difference :** $R - S = \{X R \text{ et } X S\}$

The difference is an operation on two relationships R1 and R2 having the same pattern and building a third relationship in which the tuples consist of only those located in the R1 relationship. Notation: R1 - R2

R	A	B	C
	a	e	f
	a	b	c
	d	e	g
	f	i	j

S	A	B	C
	a	b	c
	d	e	g
	a	j	k

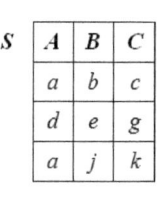

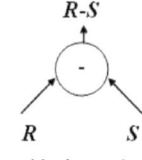

Graphical notation

- **projection :** $\Pi_{\text{liste de colonnes}}(R)$ *(No redundancy)*

Is a unary operation of deleting columns (attributes) of the table and by eliminating duplicate tuples (if an attribute of the primary key has been deleted). Projecting a pattern table of R (a1, a2 ... ap, ap + 1 ... an) in the direction (a1, a2 ... ap) is a schema S table (a1, a2 ... ap) whose tuples are those R which are deleted attributes do not belong to the projection direction and by eliminating duplicate tuples:

R	A	B	C
	a	b	c
	a	b	d
	a	c	e
	a	b	e
	a	c	f

$\prod_{A,B}(R)$

	A	B
	a	b
	a	c

$\prod_{A,B}(R)$

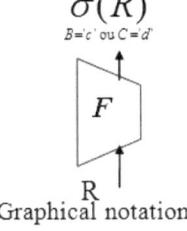
Graphical notation

- **the selection :** $\sigma_{formule}(R) = \{X \in R \ / X \text{ vérifie la formule}\}$

Restricting (or selection) of a table according to a criterion of R or Q qualification restriction (which may include one or more attributes of R) is a unary operation. Its result is an R table! The same scheme as R, R tuples are tuples verifying the qualification Q.

R	A	B	C
	a	b	c
	a	b	d
	a	c	e
	a	b	e
	a	c	f

$\sigma(R)$
$B='c' \text{ ou } C='d'$

	A	B	C
	a	b	d
	a	c	e
	a	c	f

$\sigma(R)$
$B='c' \text{ ou } C='d'$

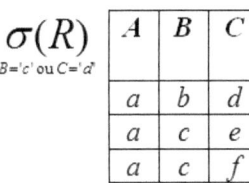
Graphical notation

- **Cartesian product:** $R \times S = \{(X, Y) / X \in R, Y \in S\}$

It's binary operation, the Cartesian product of R 2 tables and diagrams any S is a table T having the attributes concatenating those of R and S, whose tuples are all a concatenation R tuple in a tuple S

R	A	B	C
	1	2	3
	7	8	9

S	D	E
	7	1
	9	2

R×S	A	B	C	D	E
	1	2	3	7	1
	1	2	3	9	2
	7	8	9	7	1
	7	8	9	9	2

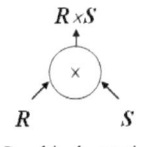
Graphical notation

- **the intersection:** $R \cap S = R - (R - S)$

It is an operation on two relationships R1 and R2 having the same pattern and building a third relationship in which the tuples consist of those belonging to the two relations.

R	A	B	C
	a	e	f
	a	b	c
	d	e	g
	f	i	j

S	A	B	C
	a	b	c
	d	e	g
	a	j	k

R∩S	A	B	C
	a	b	c
	d	e	g

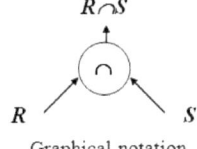
Graphical notation

- **the division :** $R \div S$

The quotient of the division of a table D (a1, a2 ... ap, ap + 1 ... an) by the sub table (ap ... an) is the Q table (a1, a2 ... ap) whose tuples are those concatenated to any of tuple give D tuple

- It allows you to search in a table subtables that are complemented by those of another table
- It provides answers to the queries form "for every x, find it"

Is $R(A_1,, A_n)$ and $S(A_{p+1},, A_n)$ with $p<n$.
$R \div S = \{X \ (A_1,, A_p) / \forall YS, \ (X, Y)R \}$

R	B	C	D	E
	a	b	c	d
	a	b	e	f
	b	c	e	f
	e	d	c	d
	e	d	e	f
	a	b	d	e

S	D	E
	c	d
	e	f

$R \div S$	B	C
	a	b
	e	d

R % S

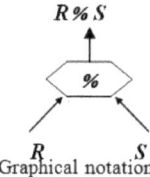

R   S
Graphical notation

Example : (fournisseur, produit) ÷ produit = Vendors selling all products.

- *the join:* $R \underset{\text{formule}}{\|} S = \{(X,Y), X R, Y S \ /(X,Y) \text{ vérifie la formule} \}$

This is a binary operation, the join tables R and S 2 is a table T obtained as follows:

1. achieve the Cartesian product of two tables R and S

2. performing a selection operation (or qualification) between an attribute of the R table and an attribute of the S table called "join attributes"

3. Whether or not to projection operation to reduce the pattern of the resulting table

Note :

1. it performs concatenation tables limited to tables of instances with common values on join attributes

2. it materializes the link between multiple tables or merging multiple tables

3. selection-qualification or "join operator" is generally equal, but can be extended to any logical operators.

4. it can be done on any attribute, without prejudging the semantic relevance of the result, only the Equality knuckle built on the primary key attributes reflect relationships (conceptual).

Is binary-operation, the join of table 2 R and S as a condition is to bring tuples tables 2 R and S to form a third table T which contains the set of all the tuples obtained by concatenating a tuple of R and S tuple satisfying condition

R	A	B	C
	1	2	3
	4	9	6
	7	8	9

S	D	E
	7	1
	9	2

$R \bowtie_{B<D} S$

A	B	C	D	E
1	2	3	7	1
1	2	3	9	2
7	8	9	9	2

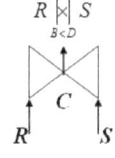

Graphical notation

- **The natural join :** $R \Join S$ *(Special case with equality on common tuples)*

The natural join of two tables R and S T is a table whose attributes are the union of R and S attributes whose tuples are obtained by concatenating a tuple of R and S tuple having same values for attributes the same name:

R	A	B
	1	2
	3	2
	1	5
	1	6

S	B	C
	2	1
	2	4
	5	1

$R \Join S$

A	B	C
1	2	1
1	2	4
3	2	1
3	2	4
1	5	1

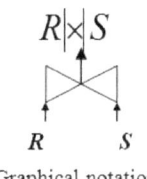

Graphical notation

3.2. Expression of the relational algebra

Algebraic operations can be combined to form expressions of relational algebra.

example:

Either the database composed of the following relationships:

R (doctor, disease rates);

S (number, ill, illness);

Doctor	Disease	Rate
Ali	bronchitis	100
Ali	tuberculosis	150
Redha	cold	300
Akile	cold	450
Mohamed	diabetes	1000

R

Number	Sick	Disease
1	Khaled	bronchitis
1	Khaled	tuberculosis
100	Omar	cold
100	Yazid	cold
7	Rasheed	diabetes

S

The answer to the question "what are the names of the doctors can examine the patient Khaled and price consultations" can be expressed using one of the following two trees:

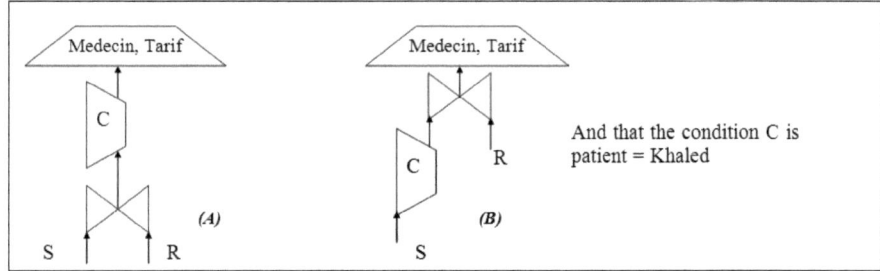

And that the condition C is patient = Khaled

An operations tree interpreter upwards. Algebraic expressions corresponding to each of the previous two shafts are respectively:

(A) $\prod_{Medecin, Tarif}(R)(\sigma_{Malade='khaled'}(R||S))$

(B) $\prod_{Medecin, Tarif}\left(R||\sigma_{Malade='khaled'}(S)\right)$

4. Standardization
4.1. functional dependence
4.1.1. Introduction
There are 5 normal forms, which are formal tests of validity and consistency of the database. Generally, we stop at the 3rd normal form. The definition of normal forms is based on the functional dependencies between different attributes of the database [1, 7].

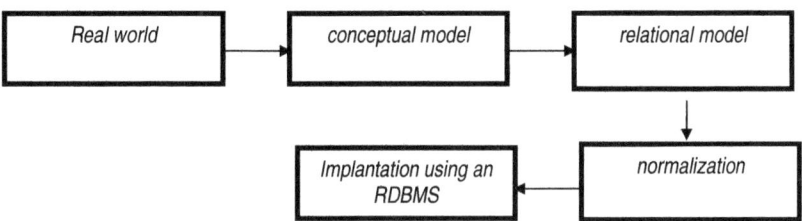

4.1.2. Definition
Is a relationship $R(A,B,C,)$. A determines B or B functionally dependent on A if and only if $a=a' \Rightarrow b=b'$ That is to say, for any value of A is a single value of B. Note A $\Box$ B.

R	A	B	C
	a	y	u
	b	c	d
	a	c	d
	f	c	d
	h	u	v

$AT \to B$ is wrong, but $B \to C$ may be true.

example:

R (UV, Day, Hour, Hall, Teacher); F = {Day, Hour, Room→UV Teacher}.

4.1.3. Graphical representation of functional dependencies
This is a graphical representation for visualizing easily all functional dependencies.

example:

Consider the following functional dependencies:

Student, Module → teacher

Student, Module → room

Prof, Module → hour

Teacher → office

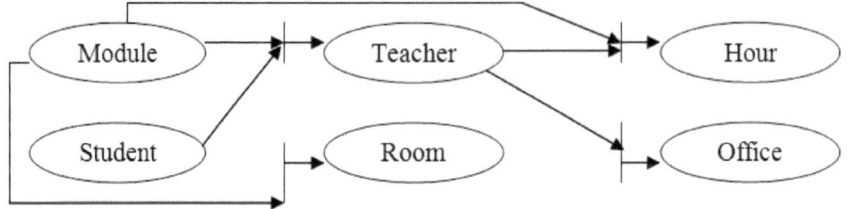

4.1.4. Properties (Armstrong axioms)

- *reflexivity:* $\forall Y X, X \to Y$
- *increase:* $X \to Y \Rightarrow XZ \to YZ$
- *transitivity* $(X \to Y \text{ et } Y \to Z) \Rightarrow X \to Z$
- *union:* $(X \to Y \text{ et } X \to Z) \Rightarrow X \to YZ$
- *pseudo-transitive:* $(X \to Y \text{ et } W Y \to Z) \Rightarrow WX \to Z$
- *decomposition :* $(X \to Y \text{ et } Z Y\ ) \Rightarrow X \to Z$

4.1.5. elementary functional dependence

DFE is called a DF of the form X→A, where A is a single attribute and A⊄X, such as $\forall\ Y \subset X$, there is no DF Y → AT.

example:

If we consider the two DF: Number, Name → Address (1) and number → Address.

(1) is a non-elemental number for DF ∈(Number, name) and there are the number DF → Address.

4.1.6. direct functional dependence

DFD is called a DF of the form X→A, where A is a single attribute and A⊄X such that: if there is no such attribute Z: X → Z and Z → AT.

example:

Or R (A, B, C, D); F = {A→B, B→C, A→C, D→B}.

AT→C is not straightforward because C is transitively dependent on A by applying the DFS A→B and B→C.

4.2. The transitive closure

Let F be a set of functional dependencies. The transitive closure F + is the set of all F dependency increased from that obtained by the above properties.

We notice $F \Leftrightarrow G$ if and only if $\dfrac{+\iota = G^\iota}{F^\iota}$.

4.3. The minimum coverage

Let F be a set of functional dependencies. G is a minimum coverage F if G is minimal, $\dfrac{+\iota = G^\iota}{F^\iota}$ and $+\iota\ \forall G^\iota G, G \supseteq F^{+\iota}$.

F minimum coverage is called a set G equivalent to F that satisfies the following three properties [5, 6]:

1. All the right parts are reduced to a single element,

2. No left side contains redundant element:

$\forall X \rightarrow AT \in G$ and $Z \subset X (G - \{X \rightarrow AT\} \cup \{Z \rightarrow A\}) \neq G^+$

3. There are no superfluous dependence:

$\forall X \rightarrow AT \in G (G - \{X \rightarrow A\}) \neq G^+$

An algorithm of (there's always at least one) minimum coverage is to "impose", in order, these three conditions:

• Step 1: It expands the X dependencies→ A1 ... An X→ A1, ..., X→Year. This gives F '.

• Step 2: For each left of F ', selecting an order of consideration of attributes and we try to remove them. Successive cuts lead to F ".

• Step 3: We choose a review about F " and seeking to remove each of the considered dependencies. Successive cuts lead to G, the final result.

example:

Either the current relationship (teacher module, room, time) checking the DF suuivantes

F = {Prof, modulus →room ; module room→hour ;

Prof, module, time →module; teacher module room→hour room}

no 1

F = 1- Prof, modulus →room   2- module, room →hour
     3- Teacher module, hour →module   4- teacher module room→hour
     5- module, room→room

no 2

F " = 1- Prof, modulus →room   2- module, room →hour
       3- Teacher module, hour →module

no 3

G = 1- Prof, modulus →room   2- module, room →hour

4.4. Closure of a set of attributes
4.4.1. Definition

The closure of a set of attributes X and denoted X + is a set of attributes such as $X + = \{ \cup Ai / X \rightarrow Ai$ can be deduced from F by applying the axioms of Armstrong}

4.4.2. A closure algorithm

Let F be a set of dependencies and $X \subseteq U$ a set of attributes [1].

The algorithm calculates a sequence of sets of attributes X (0), X (1). . .

Algorithm

Data: X, U, F

1. X (0) = X.

2. $X (i + 1) = X (i) \cup \{AT / \exists Z: Y \rightarrow Z \in$ Feta cheese $\in Z$ and $Y \subseteq X (i)\}$.

3. If X (i + 1) = X (i), the algorithm stops.

Note: The algorithm always stops since $X(0) \subseteq X(1) \subseteq X(2) ... \subseteq U$ and U is a finite set.

example:

Let F = {AB → C, D → EG, C → A BE → C, BC → D, CG → BD, ACD → B, CE → AG};

X: BD and U: ABCDEG

The algorithm calculates: X (0): BD

X (1): BDEG

X (2): BDEGC

X (3): BDEGCA

X (4): BDEGCA

4.5. Research Process key candidates

1. For df X→are checked by calculating R X +
2. If X + X = U place in a table of potential key Pc
3. If X + X ≠ U place in a table of potential key CpA by increasing
4. For X CpA the table, remove the X CpA table, for any part of U p + X, with X increasing p and let X = X∪p this set. Reapply the steps 1, 2 and 3 to X '.
5. Repeating step 4 until the table becomes empty CpA
6. Remove from the table the elements that do not meet the conditions of a key.

example:

Or R (A, B, C, D, E) satisfying the FDs:

AB→ C

C→D

BC→AT

D→AC

E→B

Step 1 : {AB} = {+ ABCD} ≠ U

{C}$^+$ ADC = {} ≠ U

{BC}$^+$= {} BCAD ≠ U

{D} = {+} DAC ≠ U

{E}$^+$ EB = {} ≠ U

Step 2 and 3: build a list of of potential key by potential key and the list increasing

	CP	CPA	**Step 4:**
We work with the elements		AB	of the list CpA
D Case: D removing table		C	CpA
Let Y = U-D + = BE .We must increase D and BE and reapply for and 3		BC	{ABCDE} - {ACD} = {} with parts of Y are B, E each increase in steps 1, 2
		D	
		E	

Together	increase by	Calculation of X +	Decision to make
DB	B	{DB} = {+} DBAC ≠ U	Add DB CpA
OF	E	{DE} = {+} = U DEACB	Add DE to Pc
DBE	BE	DBE {} = {+} = U BDEAC	Add to DBE Pc

	CP			CPA
1.	BE	A	Eliminated because contains 7	
2.	CB	E	Eliminated because contains 3	
3.	HIS	T		
4.	EB	C	Eliminated because contains 3	
5.	F	O	Eliminated because contains 5	
6.	EB	D		
7.	A	E	Eliminated because contains 7	
8.	AC	E	Eliminated because contains 7	
9.	RTS	A	Eliminated because contains 7	
10.	DA	E	Eliminated because the same 5	
11.	D	E	Eliminated same as 3	
12.	C	E	Eliminated because contains 3	
13.	DC	E		

The actual candidate keys: CE, DE and EA

4.6. poor design

Poor design of the database generates a set of problems.

example:

Either extending the next owner relationship:

Owner

NS	Name	First name	Date-purchase	Price	M	Mark	Type	Boost	court
100	Redha	Lazhar	02/10/95	10000	00019540	SEAT	Ibiza	6	R
100	Redha	Lazhar	06/11/00	50000	00010040	Opel	Corsa	9	V
400	Ali	Taha	?	?	?	?	?	?	?
?	?	?	?	?	00011040	SEAT	Leon	7	NOT
200	Nabil	Ahmed	20/04/12	5000	00011240	Citroën	2CV	2	B
200	Nabil	Ahmed	08/20/14	20000	00011440	Citroën	AM18	5	B

This table has several problems (anomalies):

Data redundancy: each person appears many times it has cars (Redha Nabil).

These redundancies can cause data inconsistency when a change:

For example, if you change the address Redha must modify all records Redha.

It is essential to use NULL in the case of people who do not own a car.

In conclusion ; This is the result of poor design: it took three relationship (person has car) instead of one.

The approach by decomposition:

The decomposition approach is a methodological approach to the design of relational patterns.

It consists from a universal relation (all attributes) and break it down into several relationships that most problems arise.

This breakdown should be performed by a decomposition algorithm and from an understanding of the semantic properties of the data.

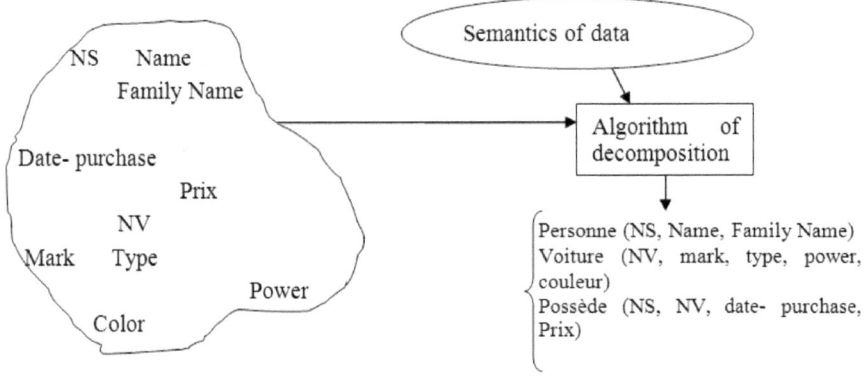

4.7. The decomposition
4.7.1. Definition
Is the replacement operation of a relation R (A1, A2, ..., An) with a set of relations R1, R2, ..., RM where each RI is obtained by a projection operation of R and such that the natural join of relations R1, R2, ..., RM (R1 ∞ R2 ... ∞ RM) gives a relation R 'having the same pattern as the relationship R. relationship can therefore decomposed in different ways. [6]

example:

Car (M brand, type, capacity, color)

M	Mark	Type	Power	Color
0666601240	SEAT	IBIZA	6	blue
0999601440	SEAT	IBIZA	6	Red

Decomposition 1:

r1 (M, type, color)

M	Type	Color
0666601240	IBIZA	blue
0999601440	IBIZA	Red

r2 (Type, Brand, Power)

Type	Mark	Power
IBIZA	SEAT	6

r1 ∞ r2 (M, brand, type, capacity, color) same pattern car.

So it is a decomposition.

r1 ∞ r2

M	Mark	Type	Power	Color
0666601240	SEAT	IBIZA	6	blue
0999601440	SEAT	IBIZA	6	Red

decomposition 2

R1 (M Type)

M	Type
0666601240	IBIZA
0999601440	IBIZA

R2 (type, power, color)

Type	Power	Color
IBIZA	6	blue
IBIZA	6	Red

R3 (type, brand)

Type	Mark
IBIZA	SEAT
IBIZA	SEAT

R1 ∞ R2 ∞ R3 has the same pattern as car so it's good decomposition.

R1 ∞ R2

M	Type	Power	Color

0666601240	IBIZA	6		blue
0666601240	IBIZA	6		Red
0999601440	IBIZA	6		blue
0999601440	IBIZA	6		Red

Let $t = R1 \bowtie R2$

$t \bowtie R3$

M	Mark	Type	Power	Color
0666601240	SEAT	IBIZA	6	blue
0666601240	SEAT	IBIZA	6	Red
0999601440	SEAT	IBIZA	6	blue
0999601440	SEAT	IBIZA	6	Red

Note

$r1 \bowtie r2 = $ car

$R1 \bowtie R2 \bowtie R3 \neq $ car

The decomposition (r1, r2) allows to find all the information by joint while the decomposition (R1, R2, R3) does not find the color of a car.

Therefore, it is necessary to introduce the concept of decomposition lossless and loss of information.

4.7.2. Decomposition Lossless Information

Decomposition of R a R 1 and R 2 is SPI if at least one of the following two DF belongs to F +

1. R1∩R2→R1-R2

2. R1∩R2→R2-R1

example:

Or R (A, B, C) satisfying F = {C→AT ; B→C} and is broken down as follows: R1 (A, C) and R2 (B, C), were R1∩R2 = {C}; R1-R2 = {A}; one notices that the DF C→AT∈F + therefore this decomposition is SPI.

4.7.3. Decomposition without loss of DF

Decomposition (R1 ... Rm) R preserves FDs (SPD) if the transitive closure of R FDs is the same as the transitive closure of the union of the Dfs R1 ... Rm.

example:

Or CAR (No. VEH, TYPE, COLOR, BRAND, POWER) and

F = {N ° VEH→ TYPE, COLOR

   TYPE → BRAND, POWER}

example:

1) R1 (NVH, TYPE, COLOR) ⇒ F1 = {NVH → TYPE, NVH → COLOR}

R2 (type, make, THEN) ⇒ F2 = {TYPE → BRAND, TYPE → THEN}

⇒ OK

2) R'1 (NVH, TYPE) ⇒ F '1 = {NVH → TYPE}

R'2 (TYPE, THEN, COLOR) ⇒ F '2 = {TYPE → THEN}

R'3 (TYPE, MARK) ⇒ F'3 = {TYPE → MARK}

⇒ ON THE LOST DF: NVH →COLOR

4.8. Why normalize?

Standardization is useful:

- To minimize data redundancy,
- To minimize data loss,
- To limit the inconsistencies in data and
- To improve the performance of treatment [3].

4.8.1 First Normal Form

definition: A relation is in first normal form if and only if all its attributes have atomic values (not multiple, non-compound).

First normal form is denoted 1NC (1FN French).

If necessary, attributes or relationship is broken down to meet the 1NC.

4.8.2. Second Normal Form

definition: Let C be a candidate key of R and A R R attribute is in second normal form if and only if it is in 1NF and for all A such that A does not belong to C, we have C→At elementary.

Second normal form is denoted 2NC (2NF French).

A relationship can be 2NF relation to one of its key candidates and not to be compared to another.

To search for a 2NF, it is necessary beforehand to determine the *All DF* and choose a candidate key. It is recommended to find *all candidate keys* in order not to let more interesting than another.

If necessary, attributes or relationship is broken down to meet the 2NF.

A relationship with a selected candidate key reduced to a single attribute is, by definition, necessarily 2NF.

Examples:

1. Order (CustomerID, codeArticle, customer, article) with DF

customer code → customer and codeArticle → article is not in 2NF

2. Person (name, age, nombreEnfants) with DF

last name First Name →age nombreEnfants is 2NF.

3. Vendor1 (NC, ProductName, Adr, Phone, Price) with DF

NF ProductName → price and NF → Adr, Phone is not in second normal form.

Such a relationship is problematic:

Redundancy: If there are 100 products for a supplier we will repeat 100 times the name, address, phone supplier.

update problem for inserts: when you want to add a product, you must re-enter the address and phone provider.

Problem for deletions: if you remove (momentarily) the list of vendor products, while also removes the supplier.

update tuples problem: if a supplier changes of address or telephone must do this update on all 100 tuples.

solution:

Vendor1 It consists of two relationships:

Provider (NF, Adr, Tel)

Catalog (NC, ProductName, Price)

Who are second normal form

This breakdown is:

Lossless (NF is the ID of the relationship Supplier)

Without loss of functional dependence (DF are either in one or the other of the two broken relationships).

4.8.3. Third Normal Form

Definition : Let C be a candidate key of R and A and B two non-empty disjoint sets of attributes R. R is in third normal form if and only if it is in 2NF and all A and B such that A and B disjoint C, no A→ B.

The third normal form is denoted 3NF (3NF French).

A relationship can be in 3NF with respect to one of its key candidates and not to be compared to another.

If necessary, attributes or relationship is broken down to meet the 3NF.

A relation in 2NF with at most one attribute that does not belong to the selected candidate key is, by definition, necessarily 3NF.

example:

Order (OrderID, CustomerID, customer, article) with DF

OrderID → CustomerID, customer, and item

customer code → customer

Not in 3NF while Person (name, age, nombreEnfants) with DF

last name First Name → age nombreEnfants

Is 3NF.

The 3NF does not solve everything. DF outnumbered in 2NF are now taken into account, which is a positive thing. But all the DF are not.

example:

University (student, subject, teacher, note) with DF

student, material → teacher, grade and

teacher → material

Is 3NF. However, it is possible to find instances<Joseph, DBMS, Taha 5> and <Patricia, IA, Taha, 17>, which is inconsistent.

4.8.4. normal form Boyce-Codd

definition: A relationship is in normal form Boyce-Codd if and only if its candidate keys are unique sources of DF [1, 4].

The normal form of Boyce-Codd BCNF is noted (FNBC French).

If a relationship is in BCNF, it is by definition for all candidate keys.

If necessary, attributes or relationship is broken down to meet BCNF.

example:

University (student, subject, teacher, note) with DF

student, teacher □ material, notes and teacher □ material is not in BCNF while Person (name, age, nombreEnfants) with DF name, first name □ age nombreEnfants is in BCNF.

4.9 Decomposition into 3NF

Principle

From a <U, F> scheme which K is a key:

1. One seeks a minimum cover G for F,

2. Each left X G dependencies such that X→A1, ..., X→ Year, is produced under a scheme <XA1 ... An, G [XA1 ... An]>

3. If none of the patterns products contains key is added under the scheme <K, ∅>.

3NF decomposition algorithm

Entrance

<U, F>, initial schema

Data structure

S, set of pairs <U, F>

Exit

final value of S: the collection of sub patterns

Algorithm

1) G: = couverture_minimale (F);

2) S: = ∅ ;

forall X X telque → A1, ..., X → Year

(Ie either the subset of G DF left X)

make

S: S = ∪{<XA1 ... An, G [XA1 ... An]>};

fact ;

3) if no element of S contains key

so

K: = a key;

S: S = ∪{<K, {∅}>};

endif;

Remarks

1. It is made from a minimum coverage which ensures that sub patterns obtained are in 3NF.

2. The preservation of dependencies is, from G, trivial.

3. It is adding a key that ensures the validity of the decomposition.

4. Simplification: without changing the general properties of the algorithm, we can simplify the result S removing all content under scheme in another scheme under S. This step is not necessary, but it simplifies the result by eliminating redundancies.

Examples

• The transportation base: <R (f, city, free), F {f → city, town → fresh, f → fresh}>

1) G = {f → city, town → fresh}

2) S = {<f city, {f → city}>, <cool city, town { → fresh}>}

3) The key f is used in S; nothing is added

• U = {class, Prof, Time, Hall, Student, Training}

F = {C → P, HS → C HP → S EC → F ET → S}

1) F is minimal.

2) gives Δ= {CP, HSC, HPS, CEF, HES}.

3) There is nothing to add.

4.10. valid decomposition BCNF

Principle

For valid decomposition with sub patterns in BCNF, we start with an initial scheme <U0, F0>. If it is not in BCNF is going to break into two patterns and then we will iterate the process on each of the patterns obtained. therefore establishes a binary tree of successive breakdowns. The strict reduction of the number of attributes of a step on the other ensures termination on each of the branches.

BCNF decomposition algorithm

Entrance

<U0, F0>, initial scheme

Data structure

X, set of pairs <U, F>

Exit

final value of X: the collection of sub patterns

Algorithm

BCNF procedure (U: attributes, F: dependency);
beginning
if <U, F> in BCNF
so
X: X = ∪{<U, F>}
if not
or X→ AT ∈ F +, X containing no key;
BCNF (XA, F [XA]);
BCNF (U -, F [U - A])
fSI
end;
X: = ∅ ;
BCNF (U0, F0);

example:

Let the relation R (number, name, specialty, city) checking DF:

Number → name

City → specialty

The key is (number, city)

R is in 1NF

first decomposition

Relationship	Key	DF	FN
R1 (city, specialty)	city	City → specialty	BCNF
R2 (number, city name)	(Number, city)	Number → name	1NF

second breakdown

Relationship	Key	DF	FN
R21 (number, name)	city	Number → name	BCNF
R22 (number, city)	(Number, city)	∅	BCNF

4.11. Decomposition without loss of information: Ullman algorithm

This algorithm checks whether a decomposition (R1, ..., Rn) with n >= 2 a relation R (A1, ..., An) satisfying a set of DF F is a decomposition without loss of information or not [5, 13, 14].

4.11.1. Formalism of the algorithm:

Ullman function (F (R1, ..., Rk), (A1, ..., An))

Entrance :
- F: DF set
- (R1, ..., Rk) decomposition
- (A1, ..., An) list of attributes R

Exit :
- Ullman = true if decomposition is Lossless
- Ullman = false if decomposition is lossy

beginning
- Mat build a matrix (k, n)
- Mat in column j (k, n) corresponds to the attribute Aj R
- Mat in row i (k, n) corresponds to the relation Ri decomposition

Fill of the matrix MAT (k, n) as follows
At the intersection of a row i and a column j to
If Aj R attribute belongs to Ri scheme
    Then place the symbol aj
Otherwise place bij symbol;
again ← true ;
While still true to =
    Ya_Eu_Changement ← false;
    DF set a course about F
    As long as there remains a DF to examine and yet true to =
        Take a DF X→Y F;
        Select two rows in Mat
        If X in the column (or columns X if X is compound)
        The 2 line have identical symbols
        Then / * transform the symbols of the Y column of these two lines as follows * /

```
            Ya_Eu_Changement ← true ;
            If one of the two symbols is a symbol aj
                    Then replace the other by aj
                    / * 2 symbols bij type * /
                    both by bij or blj
                End if
                End if
        End while
        Yes ∃ Matt filled in a line of symbols aj
                then Ullman ←true ; again← false;
        Otherwise if Ya_Eu_Changement = true
                then Ullman ←false; again← false;
        End if
End if
End while
```

end Ullman

4.11.2. Sample Application

Let the relation R (number, name, city, specialty) satisfying the following DF:

F = {city→specialty; number→name} and is the following decomposition of R:

{R1 (city, specialty); R2 (number, name); R3 (number, city)}

Step 1 : The matrix building

	Number	Name	City	Specialty
R1	b11	b12	a3	a4
R2	a1	a2	b23	b24
R3	a1	b32	a3	b34

2nd step : We choose a DF such city→specialty

Note that only R1 and R3 have the same symbol on the city column (a3). So we must make a change in the specialty column. So we change the R3 line b34 symbol a4. we will have

	Number	Name	City	Specialty
R1	b11	b12	a3	a4
R2	a1	a2	b23	b24
R3	a1	b32	a3	a4

No symbol lines have made, we move to another DF.

DF is chosen issue→name

Note that only R2 and R3 have the same symbol on the column number (a1) .We must make a change in the Name column. So we change the R3 line symbol b32 by a2.On will:

	Number	Name	City	Specialty
R1	b11	b12	a3	a4
R2	a1	a2	b23	b24
R3	a1	a2	a3	a4

Note that we have a line composed R3 only have symbols. It is concluded that decomposition occurs without loss of information.

5. The SQL Language

It is a language supplied with all commercialized relational DBMS. This is a standard recognized by the IS0 from 87 (standard so portability). It is in version 2 (SQL92) and version 3 is released soon. SQL is a DDL and DML. It is also used to define views, access rights, physical schema manipulation [6, 11].

Note: almost all the examples relate to the following scheme

MOVIE (TITLE, COUNTRY, YEAR, DIRECTOR)

DISTRIBUTION (TITLE, ACTOR)

CINEMA (NAMECINE STREET, TEL)

CINESALLES (NAMECINE, ROOM, NBPLACES)

PROGRAM (NAMECINE, ROOM, TITLE, WEEK NBENTREES)

5.1. Basic Structure

A simple SQL query has the form:

$$\text{Select } A1, ..., An$$
$$\text{From } r1, ..., rm$$
$$\text{Where } P$$

Ai are attributes, rj are relationships and P is a predicate names.

This query is equivalent to $\pi A1, ..., An\ (\sigma P\ (r1\ x\ ...\ x\ rm))$

Select clause 5.1.2

The SELECT clause ensures projection of relational algebra.

To list all the directors of the films:

    Select director

    From movie

The use of the asterisk (*) selects all the attributes of the relationship:

    Select *

    From movie

SQL returns default duplicates. To force it to eliminate, using the DISTINCT clause: select distinct director

    From movie

SELECT can be used arithmetic expressions and the renaming of attributes:

  * AS Select Prix_HT 1.17 Price includes VAT

  Fromproduit

5.1.3. Where clause

It represents the selection predicate in relational algebra. The condition regarding the attributes of the relations that appear in the FROM clause

    Select distinct director

    From movie

Where director = "Samir" and Actor = "Ahmed"

SQL uses the connectors and, or and not. To simplify the WHERE clause, you can use the entre clause.

Select Num

From account

Where balance entre 0 and 10000

5.1.4. The From clause

The from clause is the Cartesian product of the relational algebra.

The title and the director of the films programd in Dzair Algiers.

Select Title, Director

From movie, program

Where movie.Title = program. Title and program.NameNAMECine = "Dzair"

5.1.5. The variables tuples

They are defined in the FROM clause

Select Title, director

From movie as f, p program as

Where f. Title = p. Title and p.nameCine = "dzair"

Either emp (id, name, id_chef)

Select el.name, e2.name have name_chef

From emp el, emp e2

Where el.id_chef = e2.id

5.1.6. The Order by clause

Sql to sort query results

Select*

From program

Where nameCine = "dzair"

Order byhoraire asc, desc title

5.1.7 set operators

Select ...

...

Union / Intersect / except

Select ...

Note These operations eliminate duplication, in order to keep the use instead intersect all ... If t appears m times in r and n times in s then it appears:

- ➢ M + n times in r union all s
- ➢ Min (m, n) times in r intersect all s
- ➢ Max (0, m - n) times in r except all s

5.2. The aggregate functions

These are functions that act on sets (multi-sets) values:

        Avg: the average value of all

        Min: minimum value

        Max: the maximum value

        Sum: the total value of all

        Count the number of overall value

    Select count (title) from program

This query returns the number of films screened in Algiers.

Note : the same title may be counted several times if it is programed at different times and in different rooms.

    Select count (as distinct) from program

5.2.1 aggregates and group by

The number of films programd in each room:

    Select nameCine, count (as distinct)

    from program

    Group by nameCine

The attributes that appear in the select clause outside of aggregate must be involved in the group by clause

5.2.2. Aggregates and the having clause

Rooms where are programd over 3 movies:

    Select nameCine, count (as distinct)

    From program

    Group by nameCine

    Having count (as distinct)> 3

The predicate associated with having clause is tested after formation of groups defined in the group by clause.

5.2.3. nested queries

Sql provides a mechanism for nested queries. A sub query is a sql query (select-from-where) that is included in another query. She appears in the where clause of the first request.

The films programd in dzair not programd Chelia

    Select title

    from program

    Where nameCine = "dzair" and not as in (

        Select title

        from program

        Where nameCine = "Chelia")

Find accounts whose balances exceed the account balances of taha:

Account (num, balance nametit)
    Select *
    from account
    Where balance> all (
        Select balance
        from account
        Where nametit = "taha")

By replacing all by Some yields accounts whose balances are greater than the balance of at least one account taha.

Cinemas that pass all the films programd in dzair
    Select nameCine
    From program ft
    Where not exists (
        (Select distinct title
        from program
        Where nameCine- "dzair")
        except
        (Select distinct title
        From P2 program
        Where pl.nameCine p2.nameCine =))

Testing for duplicates

The unique clause to test whether a sub query contains duplicates.

The titles of films programd in one room and one times
    Select p. Title
    From program p
    Where single (
        Select pl. Title
        From p1 program
        Where p. Title = s title)

The derived relationship

    Holder (name, address)
    Account (num, balance nametit)

Give the average account balance of each person with an average balance> 1000
    Select nametit, soldemoyen
    from (
        Select nametit, avg (balance)
        from account

Group by nametit)

As result (nametit, soldemoyen)

Where soldemoyen> 1000

Note that we could have expressed this request using the having clause

5.2.4. The views

Equivalent to an access request. A view can be considered any relationship when expressing queries. A view is a virtual relationship in the sense that it does not actually contains "tuples". They help define virtual relationships for the purpose of:

- ➢ Hide certain information to users,
- ➢ Facilitate the expression of certain queries,
- ➢ Improve the presentation of certain data.

A view is defined by an expression of the form:

Create view v as query

<u>Request</u> is any query expression and v is the name of the view.

Emp (nume, salary, dept, address)

Create view empgen as (

Selec t nume, dept, address

From emp)

All information provided by employees of the department 5:

Select *

from empgen

Where dept = 5

5.2.5. Changing relationships

deletion:

Delete all employees of the department 5: delete from emp

Where dept = 5

Delete the program all the films programd in dzair where one of the actors is ahmed:

Delete from program

Where nameCine = "dzair 'and exists (

Select title

from movie

Where program.tite = movie. Title and movie.acteur = "ahmed")

Delete accounts whose balance is <the average balances of all accounts:

Delete from account

Where balance <(select avg (balance) from account)

Problem : if tuples are removed one by one account of the relationship, so each removal, we have a new value avg (balance). The sql solution is to first calculate avg (balance) and then delete tuples satisfying the test without recalculating each time the new value of avg (balance).

Insertion

Insert a tuple in the relationship "Account":

    Insert into account (num, balance nametit) values (511.1000, "taha")

Or insert into account values (511.1000, "taha")

Inserts a tuple with an unknown balance.

    Insert into account values (511, null, "taha")

Or insert into account (num, nametit) values (511, "taha")

The last 2 maj are equivalent unless a default value of the balance has been specified in the table definition statement.

Suppose we created a relationship titmoy (nametit, average) which must contain the name of the bank's customers and the average account balances.

    Insert into titmoy (nametit, average)

    Select nametit, avg (balance)

    from account

    Group by nametit

Update

Add 1% to all accounts with balances of less than 500:

    Update account

    Set balance = balance * 1.01

    Where balance ≤ 500

The condition which follows the where clause can be an SQL query.

5.3. Sql as ldd

- The relationship diagram
- The areas of the attributes
- Integrity constraints
- Managing permissions
- The management of physical storage
- The indexes for each relationship

5.3.1. Areas

- **Char (n)** : Fixed-size string n
- **Varchar (n)** : Chain variable size characters but less than n
- **Int** : Integer (under a finite set of integers depends on the machine)
- **smallint**: Integer. Subset of int
- **Numeric (p, d)** : Real-coded on p digits and max of digits in part to the right of the decimal.
- **Real** : A real floating.

- **Dated** : Yyyy-mm-dd (year, month, day)
- **Time** Hh: mm: ss (hour, minute, second)

Null values (null) are possible in all areas. To declare an attribute must not be null, we must add not null

- Create customer-domain name char (20)

5.3.2. Creating tables

- the table create clause is used

    Create table account (
        Num int not null,
        int balance
        Nametit varchar (20))

- Addition of constraints

    Create table account (
        Num int not null,
        Balance int default 0,
        Nametit varchar (20),
        Primary key (num),
        Check (num> 1))

- In SQL92, if a key attribute is then it is not null.

5.3.3. Schema Manipulation

The drop table command to delete a table.

Eg drop table account.

If a view is defined on the table then has to be used

Drop table account waterfall

Alter table to change the schema of a relationship.

Example : Alter table add account date_ouverture

    Dated

    Alter table drop waterfall account balance

5.3.4. foreign key

Let person (nss, name) and car (registration number, model, owner).

"Owner" is the owner nss. This is a foreign key in the car scheme because it is a key in another schema.

Create car table (
    matricule tank (8),
    Modelechar (10)
    Propriochar (3),
    Primary key (number),
    Foreign key (owner) references person

We [delete | update] waterfall |

restrict |

Set null

)

Cascade If a person is removed, then the cars it owns are deleted.

restrict: The system rejects the removal of a person if there are cars that are attached to it. This is the default option.

Set null If a person is removed, then the owner attribute is null.

The insertion of a car can be done if the "owner" exists in person (or zero).

nulls

Employee	Name	Salary
	Taha	10000
	Redha	null

Select *

From employee

Where salary> 12000 *returns no tuple.*

Same if the condition is Where salary <8000

Select sum (salary) from employee;   *returns 10000*

Select count (salary) from employee;   *returns 2*

Select avg (salary) from employee;   *returns 10000*

Very different from select sum (salary) / count (salary) from employee count since considers therefore null it will 10000/2 = 5000.

In fact this is equivalent to: select sum (salary) / count (salary) from employees

Where salary is not null

Select count (*) from employee

Where salary is not null;   *returns 1*

Update views

(Name, salary). Suppose the person table is empty.

   Create view as gros_salaire

   Select *

   from person

   Where salary> 10000

Insert into gros_salaire values ("redha", 5000)

   The effect of this command is inserted into the person table the tuple < "redha" 5000>.

Note that if we:

Select * from big salary; it gets no tuple.

If the creation of the view option is added:

With check option then the insertion is refused.

Updates views are translated into updates of the underlying tables. The translation is not always unique. When we have several ways to translate an update then it is rejected.⇒certain views do not allow updates. It takes one relationship between the update of the view and update the table.

5.3.5. outer join

If we: ixi person car, there will be that people who have (the) car (s) that are in the result.

    Select *

    From left outer join person per car v

        It p.nss = v.proprio

This query returns as persons who have no car. These tuples have null values for fields from car. If we simply put outer join then will people without cars and cars without owner.

The join is expressed by t1 inner join t2 is provided

In the example, if we want to reach anyone and then car

    Select *

    From personne p inner join car v

        It p.nss = v.proprio

If we put right instead of left in the join, then we will have cars without people. If we do not put neither left nor right, we will have cars and people who are not in the join.

5.3.6. Mechanism of Rights

Either the person table (num, name, addr, num_serv, salary)

1. Taha can not reach people.
2. Taha can read part of people but can not change anything.
3. Taha reads one tuple (the one on) without being able to change it.
4. Taha can also change the attribute addr.
5. Taha can access the salary attribute but only between 9 am and 17h from the terminal 25.
6. Taha may modify wage if it is less than 8000.
7. Taha may change the relationship if he is responsible for the tuple num_serv he wants change.

    The fees depend on the container, context and / or content.

5.3.7. The rights in sql

    Select: privilege it takes to read a table

    Insert, delete, update: privileges to update a table.

    Insert (x), update (x): Privilege required to insert, update attribute x.

Granting and withdrawal of privileges

Grant privilege is subject to user [with grant option]

Revoke [grant option for] privilege from one user object

    restrict | cascade

Examples:

Grant all on result table to director with grant option;

Grant insert one table to SEC_1 result;

Grant select, update (points) on table result to prof_1;

Note: A user can receive the same privilege from several sources. This is useful when one of them wants to remove him.

Example Either the sequence

    A: grant select on t tobwith option grant table

    B: grant select on t tocwith option grant table

    C: grant select on t todwith option grant table

    A: revoke select one table from t b

Or b or c can only read t

5.3.8. Using Views

    Create view informations_perso

    As select *

    from employee

    Where name = user;

    Grant select, update (address)

    It informations_perso

    to public

6. Practical work in phpMyAdmin MySQL

Introduction

The purpose of this lab is to practice the management of databases. We have chosen as an example one called phpMyAdmin tool that is coded in php web interface to manage the contents of a MySQL database. [12]

principles

At the end of each year we will export all transactions in a SQL file. This is the file that will allow us to have a trace of operations to recreate our database, and which will be useful to review the lab.

To access phpMyAdmin, we use a browser (Firefox, for example), then we go to http: // localhost / phpmyadmin /. This home page to create a base.

Note :

It uses neither focus nor space in the field names in MySQL, not to complicate the query syntax.

TP 1: Creating the database

First, we create the work base. These relationships regarding student grades.

1) Using the Databases tab, create base_students basis.

2) On that basis, always using the interface (Structure tab), create tables
    - ✓ students (primary key num_etu)
    - ✓ ratings (primary key consisting of fields and the _num_etu _num_mat)
    - ✓ materials (primary key num_mat)
    - ✓ teachers (primary key num_ens; index on name_ens field)

Care should be taken carefully select the type of each field, selecting the most suitable among the types available in MySQL.

Exercise 1 :

Indicate in a table and the reasons, select properties for each field: type, size / value, default value, attributes, null allowed, index,'AUTO_INCREMENT?.

TP 2: Inserting data

The goal here is to become familiar with the software interface and study some field properties.

1) Using the Insert tab, manually enter the student number 2 (in the appropriate table). Note the presence of a space between the first and last names of the students.

Exercise 1 :

Copy and explain the request generated by MySQL at this insertion.

2) Check that the auto increment is functional in the Student table (property AUTO_INCREMENT (a_i) for num_etu key), adding the student Houcine Fatima, but this time without specifying the number.

Exercise 2:

Copy and explain the request generated by MySQL at this insertion, as well as its result.

3) Prohibit duplicates in the field name_etu (by adding a UNIQUE index in the tab Structure) and verify that this constraint is respected.

Exercise 3:
Copy and explain the message of MySQL when inserting a duplicate for the student name.

TP 3: Importing and exporting data

Here we show how to import data using the interface or an application, and how to export a complete database to another DBMS or spreadsheet.

1) Enable the students table and in the Import tab, student.csv import the file. This file is in CSV format, the column separator is the tab character (written \ t), and the columns are not surrounded by any particular character. This import is expected to generate an error!

Exercise 1 :
Explain the origin of this error, the result for the content of the Student table, and propose possible solutions to address them (make one of them).

2) Another way to import data into an existing table is to use the SQL statement:
LOAD DATA INFILE 'file' INTO TABLE table
In the SQL tab, perform in this way the import of 3 other .csv files for tables that students other. For this, you've got to copy these files to the directory containing the base (ie C: \ wamp \ bin \ mysql \ mysql5.5.24 \ data \ base_students \), which avoids to specify the file path in the LOAD request DATA.

Exercise 2:
In referring to the MySQL documentation LOAD DATA, draw a parallel between import the table students by this method and the one used in the previous question.

3) the appropriate tab, export the SQL code of the complete database (structure and data).

Exercise 3:
Learn about the SQL commands contained in the file and exported. Comment this code, particularly the structure of the CREATE TABLE query.

4) this time We are looking to export to Excel based, firstly, and to the Calc spreadsheet LibreOffice (Open Document Spreadsheet), on the other.

Exercise 4:
What format do you recommend in each case? Justify this choice when multiple solutions are possible, as in the case of export to Excel.

TP 4: Selecting Data

Here, we will practice the single-table data selection and multi-table through SQL.

Exercise 1 :

For each question,
- reproduce the code (of) application (s), explaining the key challenges, especially those that are new compared to previous requests;
- provide guidance for checking whether the result is correct, for example: number of lines, value (s) returned (s), etc.

1) Find the names and dates of birth of students born before 1994. Using two possible date formats in MySQL.

2) Find the note of Houcine student, Fatima Databases. The text fields, such as the name of the student or that of matter, are case sensitive and accent?

3) Find the number of students born in 1994. This may be done using the YEAR () function.

4) Find (if any) teachers who teach any subject. For this, we will successively make the following requests:
- find teachers as well as (the) matter (s) that each sign;
- transform join the previous query in outer join to find all the teachers, they teach or not material;
- finally remember that teachers who do not teach any subject.

5) Find the numbers, name and average students under 22 years old (or whose date of birth is unknown) who had a score in each subject, displaying the names in ascending order.

TP 5: Data Update

Here are studied new SQL clauses that allow the modification of the database.

1) See the table for teachers and, with the button, set it to 0 seniority Taha Musa.
Exercise 1 :
Copy the request generated by MySQL in this update, and deduce the syntax of this new clause.

2) inspiring you to the previous query, query for it to 0 seniority of all teachers with the MCB grade.
Exercise 2:
Copy this request. What is the number of changed lines as well?

3) Make a request put to multi-table update (see the MySQL manual if necessary) to add a point to all grades in compilation.
Exercise 3:
Copy this request and explain its syntax. What is the number of rows affected?

TP 6: Data Deletion

Apart from new SQL clauses allowing deleting data in the database, we discuss here the problem of the consistency of the data.

1) Delete the last student with the button.

Exercise 1 :

Copy the request generated by MySQL at this deletion. Conclude the syntax of this new clause.

2) inspiring you to the previous query, remove all of the students were born before 1990.

Exercise 2:

Copy this request. What problem does it arises as to the consistency of the database?

3) Develop a multi-table query to delete all information related to the student Dupont, Charles.

Exercise 3:

Copy and explain this request. What advantage does this (compared to previous) on the consistency of the database?

4) Develop a multi-table query to delete the notes of the student Dubois, Jules without removing the student himself.

Exercise 4:

Copy this request and explain its syntax by comparing it to the previous one. Is the consistency that student data preserved?

TP 7: Relations between tables

Managing relationships is a powerful mechanism to manage referential integrity of the database. It is to compel a foreign key to take one of the primary key values ("primary key") that reference. This mechanism is supported by the table InnoDB storage engine (default engine in MySQL since Version 5.5.5), subject to some conditions on the properties of foreign key fields.

1) At this point TP, the base is probably in an inconsistent state after following the instructions of TPs 5 and 6. Reset so that base by removing all of its tables, and recreating the through SQL exported in TP 3.

2) Ensure that each foreign key has the same properties (type, size, sign) that the primary key it references (make any necessary changes).

3) In the Structure tab, using the button, add an index on each non-indexed foreign key.

Exercise 1 :

What are the relevant fields (argue)?

4) By clicking on relational view, in each table, connect each foreign key to the primary key it references (leaving for now as RESTRICT strategy update and delete).

Exercise 2:

Copy and explain one of the queries generated during these manipulations, so that the message delivered by MySQL during the updating and deleting a primary key referenced (e.g., modify the teacher numeral 15 in 25, delete the teacher No. 10).

5) In the relational view of the table teachers define name_ens as descriptive column and then insert a new material using the management interface.

Exercise 3:
What changes can you see
- the display of table data subjects?
- when inserting a new material?

6) In the relational view of the materials table, apply a cascading update _num_ens the foreign key.

Exercise 4:
Copy and explain the request generated during this manipulation. What is its impact on the updating of a teacher number (eg change the teacher's number 15 at 25)?

7) Remove the teacher # 14, then # 10.

Exercise 5:
What explains the difference found in these cuts? Copy and explain the message delivered by MySQL in the second. What will happen if one opts for the cascading deletion policy and the deletion of the teacher No. 10?

8) Test all strategies (CASCADE, SET NULL, NO ACTION, RESTRICT) and their impact on the data during an update or a delete.

Exercise 6:
Make a comprehensive proposal for the full basic relationship management so that referential integrity is managed at best: which update strategies and delete do you propose for each foreign key, and any descriptive column you choose for each table ?

Exercises

Exercise 1 :
Consider the following 3 sets of DF:
F1 = {A→B; B→C}
F2 = {A→B; AT→C}
F3 = {A→B; AB→C}
1. Does F1 and F3 are equivalent?
    ➢ If so, deduct formally F3 F1 and vice versa (using Armstrong's axioms)
    ➢ If not, give an against-example, ie of a relationship that meets a set of dependencies, but not the other.
2. Same question for F2 and F3.

Exercise 2:
a) A relation R (A, B, C, D, E) satisfies the DF {ABC →DE; E→BCD}
   1. Find all the keys of R.
   2. In which normal form is R?
   3. Submit a decomposition.
   4. Is your decomposition is SPI? (Apply the algorithm Ullman).
b) Show that the following diagrams are not in 3NF:
   1. R (A, B, C, D) with functional dependencies f = {AB→C, B→D, BC→AT}.
   2. **2.** R (C, P, H, S, E, N) with the functional dependencies f = {C→P, HS→C HP→S EC→N ET→S}

Exercise 3:
Given the following relational tables:
Employee (emp_id, name, address, hire_date, #nameprojet)
Nationalities (#emp_id, nationality)
Project (Projectname, #responsable); Reference responsible Employé.emp_id
An employee can have multiple nationalities. An employee working on a project. For each project, we keep the leader who is also an employee.
   a) Write the following queries in SQL:
1. For each employee display his name and nationality.
2. For each employee of Swiss nationality, display name, first name.
3. Show for each employee's name, first name and number of nationality.
4. Display for each employee's name, project name on which he / she works and the name of its leader.
   b) Fourth rewrite the query relational algebra.

Exercise 4:
   1. Suppose two relations R (A, B) and S (A, B) with exactly the same pattern. Which of the following equalities, which one is correct in relational algebra?
      (A) R∩S = R- (HR); (B) R∩S = S- (SR); (C) R∩S = R ∞ S.
   2. Suppose two relations R (A, B) and S (A, B) with exactly the same pattern. The only key of R is A; the only S key is Also. The relationship T (A, B) represents the union of set-R and S, that is to say, T = R∪S. What are the key or T?

Exercise 5:
Consider the following relational schema:
 CUSTOMER (NumCli, Name, Email, NumCB)
 BOOKING (NumCli, CodeVoyage, DateRes)
 TRIP (CodeVoyage, Destination, Time, Price)
Formulate relational algebra the following requests:
1. Full name and email customers with current reservation
2. Full name and email customers with no current reservation
3. Destination and list of customers who booked for a trip of more than 10 days and costing less than 1,000 dinars.
4. Numbers of all customers who booked on all the trips offered.

Exercise 6:
Consider a relation R (Host, Sports, Location, Group, Schedule).
And F = {A → S; A, C→G; C,→AT ; C, G→ L}.
1. From the interpretation of DF F, answer the following questions:
- Can some moderator teach different sports?
- Can a given host supervise different groups?
- two different sports can they take place simultaneously in the same place?
2. We have G = {A →S; A, C→L; C,→G; C, G→AT}. Are the sets F and G equivalent? Making a formal demonstration using the axioms of Armstrong.
3. Offers a primary key for the relation R.
4. In what normal form is the relation R?
5. Leave a detour R decomposition relationships in third normal form.

Exercise 7:
Consider the following relational model:
 CUSTOMER (codeclt, Nameclt, Fnameclt, address, PC, city)
 PRODUCT (reference, Description, price)
 TECHNICIAN (CODETEC, Nametec, Fametec, tauxhoraire)
 INTERVENTION (number, Date, reason, #codeclt, # reference #codetec)
Express in SQL the following queries:
1. The list of products (reference and designation), ranked from least to most expensive
2. The number of interventions by technician
3. The product designations for which the average price is higher than 300 DA
4. The list of customers who requested an intervention for products of a higher price to 30 DA
5. Interventions by the technician with the code 81 between July 5 and August 5, 2009

Exercise 8 (QCM):
A) A conceptual model consists of:
Connections 1- 2- 3- entities and associations tables
B) At the conceptual level, what is the name of the highlighted properties?
1- primaires2- key identifiers 3- foreign keys

C) What does an entity physically?
1- to 3- relation 2- an association to a table
D) The relational level can identify:
1- identifiants 2- the foreign key tables 3-

Exercise 9:

R and S are relations:

R	
A	B
at	b
at	f
c	b
d	e

S	
B	C
b	c
e	at
b	d
g	b

Where the attributes A, B, C are defined in the fields of letters of the alphabet.

Write the result of the following requests:

(Rennomage) $S2 = \rho_{B:\ D}(S)$; $R \times S2$; $R \infty S$; (semi join) $R \propto S = \pi_R(R \infty S)$; $S1 = \rho_{IT}(S)$; $R \cap S1$; $R \cup S1$; R-S1; S1-R.

Exercice 10:

Let the next person relationship:

Name	Age	City
Fatima	29	Alger
Redha	32	Batna
Zayneb	54	Alger
Nour	13	Khenchela
Taha	40	Batna

A) Write the results of the following requests:

$\sigma_{age=30}$(no one) ; π_{age}(no one) ; $\pi_{age}(\sigma_{name='Serge'}$(no one)) ;

B) Express the following queries in relational algebra:

1. The people (name, age, city) living Algiers.
2. The people (name, age, city) who are under 30 years.
3. Cities PERSON relationship.
4. The names of the people living in Algiers.

exercise 11 :

Let the employee relationship (EWB) and the relationship department (dept) below:

	ENO	ENAME	TEACHER	DATEEMB	SAL	COMM	DNO
EMP	10	Ali	Engineer	01/10/93	4000	3000	3
	20	Redha	Technician	05/01/88	3000	2000	2

	30	Taha	Seller	03/01/80	5000	5000	1
	40	Yacine	Engineer	03/01/80	5000	5000	3

	DNO	DNAME	DIR	CITY
	1	Commercial	30	Khenchela
DEPT	2	Production	20	Batna
	3	Development	40	Setif

A) Write the results of the following requests:

$\sigma_{sal < 5000}(EMP)$; $\pi_{ENO, COMM}(EMP)$;

B) expressed by a sentence that is obtained by evaluating the previous queries.

C) What is the expression of relational algebra that would get the name and occupation of the employee number 10.

D) Same for the names of employees who work in Khenchela.

E) Same for the name of the director of the department "Commercial".

Exercise 12:

Build relational schemas from entity-relationship diagrams presented below.

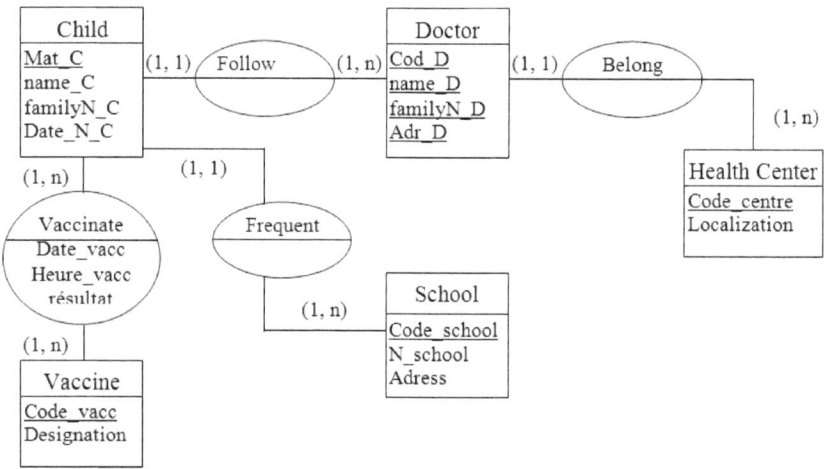

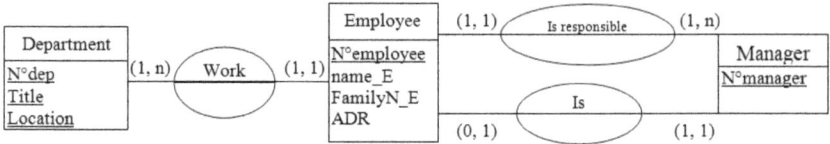

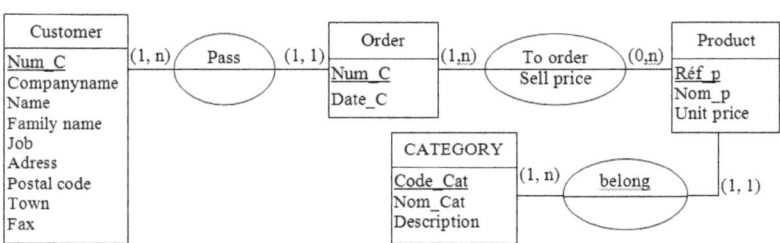

Exercise 12:
Either the pattern R (A, B, C, D, E) and the relation r. What functional dependencies are not met by r?

r

A	B	C	D	E
a1	b1	c1	d1	e1
a1	b2	c2	d2	e1
a2	b1	c3	d3	e1
a2	b1	c4	d3	e1
a3	b2	c5	d1	e1

Note: Recognize the Functional Dependencies met on r tuples does not prove that these dependencies exist on R.

Exercise 2:
Or R (A, B, C, D, E, G, H) and F = {AB→C, B→D CD→E, EC→GH, G→AT}. Did you:
AB→E? BG→C? AB→ G?
- Answer using the axioms of Armstrong.
- Answer by computing transitive closures of the attributes of the left portion of the DF.

Exercise 13:
1 The two sets of functional dependencies F and G are they the same?
F {A→B, CE→H, C→I,→CH} and G = {C→EH A→BC}
1 F-it is minimal?
2 Calculate a minimum coverage F
3 What are the candidate keys of F?

Exercise 14:

Considering the relation R (A, B, C, D, E, F) on which are defined the following functional dependencies:

A, B → C
D → C
D → E
C, E → F
E → AT

A	B	C	D	E	F
	1		110		54
x	2	j	100	not	52
w	1	i	110	m	
	2		100		52

1. Fill in the blanks of the table:
2. Calculate the closing of the following sets of attributes:
(A) {D} +
(B) {A, B} +
(C) {C, E} +
3. Give the candidate keys of the relation R.

Exercise 15:
Or the relational schema R (A, B, C, D), F = {A→B, C→ D} and decomposition Δ = {AB, CD}
1. Show that Δ is not a decomposition without loss of information.
2. Give a decomposition without loss of information.

Exercise 16:
Either the relational schema R (vendor, address, NameProd, price), F = {f→A fN→ P}
Find decomposition without loss of information.

Exercise 17:
Either the relational schema R (Store, Article, Department Head)
F = {MA→D, MD→ R}
1. Show that the only key is MA.
2. Find a decomposition without loss of information.

Exercise 18:
Either the scheme: R (A, B, C, D), F = {AB→C, B→D, C→AT}
  1. Leave a decomposition preserves the dependencies F
  2. Is this decomposition lossless?

Exercise 19:
Either the scheme: R (A, B, C, D), F = {A→B, B→CD→B} and decomposition Δ = (ACD, BD)
Is Δ F preserves dependencies

Exercise 20:
Find breakdowns in relationships that are in 3NF, decompositions that preserve the dependencies that are lossless for the following schemes:
Scheme 1: R (A, B, C, D), F = {A→B, B→C, A→D, D→C}.
Scheme 2: R (C, P, H, S, E, N), F = {C→P, HS→C HP→S EC→N ET→S}.
Scheme 3: R (F, A, N, P), F = {F→A FN→P}
Scheme 4: R (M, A, D, R), F = {MA→D, MD→R}

Exercise 21:
Either the scheme: R (A, B, C, D), F = {AB→C, B→D, C→AT}
1. Leave a lossless decomposition and preserves the dependencies F.
2. Is this decomposition is in BCNF?

Exercise 22:
Either the relationship: COURS_ETUD (student, age, courses, day_week) with the following functional dependencies:
F = {student → Ages courses → day_week}
1 Give a concrete example of this relationship (in extension, with at least 5 tuples).
2 What are the candidate keys of this relationship?
3 In which normal form this relationship is it? On your specific example, highlight the problems that can occur when handling this table.
4 Do decomposition BCNF. Is the decomposition SPI? Is she SPD?
5 Apply the decomposition to your specific example. then repeat the join on this example and make sure you get good starting relationship.

Exercise 23:
Spend the following relation in 1NF. Add the contents of the inferred relationship.

Type_avion	Capacity
CARAVEL	(100)
CONCORDE	(400, 600)
AIRBUS	(250, 275)
B707	(180, 150, 160)
B747	(350)

Exercise 24:
Sql express the following requests:
Either the relational database schema:
Plant (naked nameu, city)
Product (np, pname, color, weight)
Supplier (nf NAMEF, status, city)
PUF (np naked nf, quantity)
1. Give the number, name and city of all plants.
2. Give the number, name and city of all plants of Batna.

3. Give the numbers of suppliers that supply the plant No. 1 product 1.
4. Give the name and color of the products delivered by the No. 1 supplier.
5. Give the numbers of suppliers that supply the plant No. 1 in a red product.
6. Give the names of suppliers who supply a plant or batna of Algiers in a red product.
7. Give the numbers of the products delivered to a factory by a supplier in the same city.
8. Give the numbers of the products delivered to a mill batna by batna provider.
9. Give the numbers of plants that have at least one provider who is not in the same city.
10. Give the numbers of suppliers that supply both plants No. 1 and No. 2.
11. Give the numbers of plants using at least one product available from supplier # 3 (that is to say a product that book but not necessarily at the plant).
12. Leave the lightest product number (numbers if several products have the same weight).
13. Give the numbers of factories that receive no red produces a London supplier.
14. Give the numbers of suppliers that provide at least one product provided by at least one provider that provides at least one red product.
15. Give all triples (villef, np, Villeu) such as a supplier of the first city supplies a factory in the second city with a product np.
16. Same as Question 15, but the triplets where the two cities are identical.
17. Give the numbers of the products that are delivered to all plants of Batna.
18. Give the numbers of suppliers who supply all plants with the same product.
19. Give the numbers of factories that buy the supplier # 4 all the products it provides.
20. Give the numbers of factories that purchase only from the supplier 3.
21. Add a new provider: <45, Farid, subcontractor, khenchela>
22. Delete all black products and number between 100 and 199.
23. Change city the # 1 provider: he moved to khenchela.

Exercises Solutions
Exercise 1 :
F1 = {A→B; B→C}
F2 = {A→B; AT→C}
F3 = {A→B; AB→C}
1- No, the following table satisfied F3, but not F1

A	B	C
1	2	5
3	2	6

Yes. First we deduce F3 from F2. We have A→ C, increases were AB → CB by decomposition deduced AB → C.
In the other direction is deduced F2 from F3. We have A→ B, by increasing (by A) we obtain A →AB. with AB→C A is obtained by transitivity →C.

Exercise 2:
Since A is never in the right side of DF can not get it from other attributes, so each key contains A.

If a key does not contain E, to implement the FD is required of B and C, so the key contains ABC. Direct verification shows that from ABC everything can get, so it's a key (and no others without E).

If a key contains E, it contains AE, and one can easily get everything from AE. So the only key that contains E is EI.

Conclusion: there are two key ABC and AE.

2- course attributes are atomic and R is 1NC. DF E→ D from a clean part (E) of a key (AE) to a D attribute that belongs to no key.

Therefore R is not in 2NF. Conclusion: only 1NC.

A relation R (A, B, C, D, E) satisfies the DF {ABC →DE; E→BCD}

3- R can be decomposed into:

R1 (A, B, C, D); F1 = {ABC→D} BCNF
R2 (A, E); F1 =Ø BCNF
R3 (B, C, D, E); F1 = {E→ BCD} BCNF

4- Initial state

	AT	B	C	D	E
R1	a1	a2	a3	a4	b15
R2	a1	b22	b23	b24	at 5
R3	b31	a2	a3	a4	at 5

final state

	A	B	C	D	E
R1	a1	a2	a3	a4	b15
R2	a1	a2	a3	a4	at 5
R3	b31	a2	a3	a4	at 5

There Mat in a full line of symbols aj; thus this decomposition is SPI.

b)

1- R (A, B, C, D) with functional dependencies f = {AB→C, B→D, BC→AT}

The only two keys are AB and BC and we have B→D; key→]A key therefore is not in 2NF consequently is not in 3NF.

2-R (C, P, H, S, E, N) with the functional dependencies f = {C→P, HS→C HP→S EC→N ET→S}

The only key is HE and we have C →P;]key→]R key therefore is not in 3NF.

Exercise 3:

at)

1-select name, nationality from Employee, Nationalities Where Employee. emp_id = Nationalitys.emp_id.

2- select surname, name from employee Where Employee. emp_id = = Nationalitys.emp_id and nationality as Swiss.

3- select name, count (nationality) from Employee, Nationalities Where Employee. emp_id = Nationalitys.emp_id group by name, forename

4- E1.name select, projectname, employee E2.name from E1, E2 employed, project Where E1.nameprojet projet.Nameprojet = and = projet.responsable E2.emp_id.

b)

$\Pi_{nom, nomprojet, nomresp}$ (Employee $\bowtie_{empl_{id}=responsable}$ ((Project $\bowtie \rho$[Name: nameresp] (employee))

Exercise 4:
1- (a), (b), (c).
2 - A

Exercise 5:
Consider the following relational schema:
    CUSTOMER (NumCli, Name, Email, NumCB)
    BOOKING (NumCli, CodeVoyage, DateRes)
    TRIP (CodeVoyage, Destination, Time, Price)
Formulate relational algebra the following requests:

1. Full name and email customers with current reservation

$\Pi_{nom, prénom, e\text{-}mail}$ (BOOKING $\bowtie_{RESERVATION.NumCli = CLIENT.NumCli}$ (CUSTOMER)

2. Full name and email customers with no current reservation

$\Pi_{nom, prénom, e\text{-}mail}$ (BOOKING $\bowtie_{RESERVATION.NumCli != CLIENT.NumCli}$ (CUSTOMER)

3. Destination and list of customers who booked for a trip of more than 10 days and costing less than 1,000 dinars.

$\Pi_{Destination, nom, prénom, e\text{-}mail}$ ($\sigma_{Durée > 10 \text{ and } Prix < 1000}$ (VOYAGE) $\bowtie$ BOOKING)

4. Numbers of all customers who booked on all the trips offered.

$\Pi_{nom, prénom, e\text{-}mail}$ (CUSTOMER $\bowtie$ BOOKING $\bowtie$ TRIP)

Exercise 6:
Consider a relation R (Host, Sports, Location, Group, Schedule).
And F = {A → S; AC→G; CL→AT ; CG→ L}.
1. From the interpretation of DF F, answer the following questions:
- Can some moderator teach different sports? NO
- Can a given host supervise different groups? YES
- two different sports can they take place simultaneously in the same place? NO

2. We have G = {A →S; AC→L; CL→G; CG→AT}. Are the sets F and G equivalent? Making a formal demonstration using the axioms of Armstrong.

Yes. First F deduced from G.
AT → S ∈ G
We AC → The increase in AC → CL by transitivity with CL → G is obtained AC → G
We CL → G by increasing CL → CG by transitivity with CG → A is obtained CL → AT
We CG → A by increasing CG → CA by transitivity with AC → The CG is obtained → The
In the other direction is deduced from G to F.
AT → S ∈ F

We AC → G increase by AC → CG by transitivity with CG → The AC is obtained → The
We CL → A by increasing CL → CA by transitivity with CA → G is obtained CL → G
We CG → The increase by CG → CL by transitivity with LC → A CG is obtained → AT

3. Offers a primary key for the relation R.
C does not appear in the right part of any DF then it is part of any key; we have C + = {C}
Is increased by an attribute for example A:
{AC} = {+} = U CALGS so you can use CL as a primary key for R

4. In what normal form is the relation R?
R is not in 2NF since we have A→S part of the key determines a non-key attribute so R is in 1NF
5. Leave a detour R decomposition relationships in third normal form.
There are no redundant DFS then CM = F
R1 (A, S); F1 = {A→ S}.
R2 (A, C, G); F2 = {AC → G}.
R3 (C, L, A); F3 = {C,→ AT}.
R4 (C, G, L); F4 = {C, G → L}.
The CA key∈R3 is not added another relationship so Δ= (R1, R2, R3, R4)

Exercise 7:
Consider the following relational model:
   CUSTOMER (codeclt, Nameclt, Fameclt, address, PC, city)
   PRODUCT (reference, Description, price)
   TECHNICIAN (CODETEC, Nametec, Fametec, tauxhoraire)
   INTERVENTION (number, Date, reason, #codeclt, # reference #codetec)
Express in SQL the following queries:
1. The list of products (reference and designation), ranked from least to most expensive
   SELECT reference designation FROM PRODUCT ORDER BY ASC prices
2. The number of interventions by technician
   SELECT CODETEC, COUNT (number) FROM INTERVENTION GROUP BY CODETEC
3. The product designations for which the average price is higher than 300 DA
SELECT FROM WHERE designation price PRODUCT> 300
4. The list of customers who requested an intervention for products of a higher price to 30 DA
SELECT nameclt, Fameclt FROM CUSTOMER, PRODUCT, WHERE INTERVENTION PRODUCT. Reference = INTERVENTION. Reference and INTERVENTION.codeclt = CLIENT.codeclt and price> 300;
5. Interventions by the technician with the code 81 between July 5 and August 5, 2009
SELECT * FROM WHERE INTERVENTION Codetec = 81 and Date BETWEEN 05/07/2009 AND 05/08/2009;

Exercise 8 (QCM):
A) A conceptual model consists of entities and associations
B) At the conceptual level, the name of the highlighted properties is an identifier
C) An entity physically corresponds to a table
D) The relational level can identify foreign keys

Exercise 23:

Solution 1:

Explode the group repetitive CAPACITY creating a new tuple for each different group.

Type_avion	Capacity
CARAVEL	100
CONCORDE	400
CONCORDE	600
AIRBUS	250
AIRBUS	275
B707	180
B707	150
B707	160
B747	350

Solution 2:

Create a column for each value

Type_avion	Cp1	Cp2	cP3
CARAVEL	100	NULL	NULL
CONCORDE	400	600	NULL
AIRBUS	250	275	NULL
B707	180	150	160
B747	350	NULL	NULL

References

[1] Belattar B., Data Bases Course, University of Batna

[2] Carrez C. The structures to Databases, Masson

[3] Cornuéjols A., General on the design of a database, University of Paris-Sud

[4] P. Crescenzo, Course Databases, University of Nice Sophia Antipolis (UNS)

[5] CJ Date, An Introduction to Database Systems, Addison-Wesley

[6] Gardarin G. Mastering Databases: models and languages, Eyrolles

[7] Herman D., P. Burgevin, fresnais P., Database, an introduction to the relational model, reindeer University 1

[8] Hervet E., relational database and distributed, University of Moncton

[9] Mr Hervé, The relational model, University of Grenoble 1

[10] Marcenac, P., relational DBMS, performance optimization, Eyrolles.

[11] J. Melton and Simon AR, Understanding SQL, A Complete Guide, Morgan Kaufmann

[12] Olivier L., Information Systems for the Enterprise Steering, University of Lille 1

[13] Valluri RS Introduction to database systems, ETH Lausanne EPFL

[14] JD Ullman, Principles of Database and Knowledge-Based Systems, 2 volumes, Computer Science Press

YOUR KNOWLEDGE HAS VALUE

- We will publish your bachelor's and master's thesis, essays and papers

- Your own eBook and book - sold worldwide in all relevant shops

- Earn money with each sale

Upload your text at www.GRIN.com and publish for free